Collector's Guide to

1990s Barbie DOLLS

Identification
&
Values

Maria Martinez-Esguerra

COLLECTOR BOOKS
A Division of Schroeder Publishing Co., Inc.

The current values in this book should be used only as a guide. They are not intended to set prices, which vary from one section of the country to another. Auction prices as well as dealer prices vary greatly and are affected by condition as well as demand. Neither the Author nor the Publisher assumes responsibility for any losses that might be incurred as a result of consulting this guide.

Searching For A Publisher?

We are always looking for knowledgeable people considered to be experts within their fields. If you feel that there is a real need for a book on your collectible subject and have a large comprehensive collection, contact Collector Books.

Front cover: Costume Ball; Sparkle Eyes; All Stars Midge; All American Kira; Earring Magic; Totally Hair.

Back cover: Western Stampin'; Dance Moves Teresa; Jewel Hair Mermaid Midge.

Cover design by Beth Summers
Book design by Mary Ann Dorris

COLLECTOR BOOKS
P.O. Box 3009
Paducah, Kentucky 42002-3009

Printed in the U.S.A. by Image Graphics Inc., Paducah KY

❃ CONTENTS ❃

✲ DEDICATION ✲

For Meredith
without whom this book would not exist.

I also give a world of thanks to the two men in my life who helped me in some other ways to complete this project:

My husband, Ray, for his uncomplaining endurance and patience in picking up Barbie dolls from crowded toy stores and the post office; and

My big brother, Fernando, for lending me his camera, when I lost mine, to photograph this collection and share it with you.

I also thank everyone across the country who has given me, sold me, or traded with me a Barbie doll, and shared their doll price list with me. Most of all, I give my heartfelt thanks to all my friends in California who share my enthusiasm for doll collecting and encouraged me to write this book, and to all others who were instrumental in getting this book in print.

✻ INTRODUCTION ✻

The Many Faces of Barbie and Friends in the Nineties

This book features Mattel's regular line of "pink box" Barbie dolls and Barbie doll's friends, Midge, Christie, Teresa, Kira, and Nia, that were produced and distributed in American stores from 1989 to the present time.

The purpose of this book is to assist collectors and would-be collectors in identifying out-of-box Barbie dolls and her more "popular" friends, Midge, Christie, Teresa, Kira, Nia, and Tara Lynn, that were produced in the nineties. For ease in identification, I have arranged the dolls according to ethnicity and color of hair. Chapter 1 presents blonde Barbie and red-haired Midge. Chapter 2 shows brunette Barbie, Hispanic Teresa, and Tara Lynn; Chapter 3 introduces Black Barbie and Christie; and finally, Chapter 4 features Asian and Native American Barbie, Kira, and Nia.

This book does not cover the regular line of Barbie's other family and friends, such as Skipper or Ken. It also does not cover the special or limited edition Barbie dolls that were made by Mattel exclusively for foreign or domestic stores, such as FAO Schwarz, Toys R Us, and other department or specialty stores. There are currently several colorful picture books that feature these "Store Exclusive" or specialty, custom-made dolls.

I have chosen to write this book on the regular "pink box" Barbie dolls because these are the best play dolls that give children of all ages the most satisfaction. These dolls are combed, dressed, and re-dressed perhaps several hundred times in a matter of months. Once the doll is taken home from the store and given to a child, the box is often thrown away and the doll's name is forever forgotten.

These regular line dolls are the kind that one would also find in thrift shops, flea markets, or garage sales because a child has outgrown playing with them. Because Barbie dolls are beautiful, they are often "redeemed" from these places; they are cleaned, coifed, re-dressed, and once again recycled and played with. Some collectors have also re-dressed them in exquisite fashions and beaded, dazzling gowns, and these dolls now grace their curio cabinets! And on and on it goes. But do you know the original name of that Barbie doll? And is that the original outfit she's wearing? What about her accessories? Do you know what accessories came with that doll before she was taken out of the box? If she had been kept in the original box and not played with, what is she worth today?

It is my hope that this book will help answer those questions. Pictures are worth a thousand or more words, so I have photographed these dolls out of their boxes. Both a close-up and a full-size, head-to-toe photograph were taken of each doll so that you may see not only the detailed facial features and the position of the iris and eyelashes that make each doll unique, but also the doll's original outfit and accessories. The approximately 600 pictures shown in this book are identified by name of the doll, stock number, and the year shown on the doll's original box. Then it will be up to you to find the adjectives describing what you see in the photographs!

The values shown reflect the current average price of the doll as though it was never removed from box (NRFB), and are intended to be only a guide. They were derived by compiling and then averaging the prices quoted in several dealer catalogs, advertised price lists, doll shows, and other published price guides on Barbie dolls. Who is to say that an out-of-box Barbie doll is worth more or less than another in a box? Can you put a price tag on the happiness that a played-with doll has given the child in each of us?

In deciding whether to collect these Barbie dolls for investment or enjoyment, collectors should note that there are a lot more white Barbie dolls produced than the Black, Hispanic, Asian, or Native American Barbie dolls. Also, there are more regular line, pink box Barbie dolls produced than store exclusive dolls. The elementary law of supply and demand tells us that the more dolls of a kind there are, the more common they are, and the lower the demand and value for them. Collectors should also decide whether they want to preserve the doll in the box, or enjoy them out of the box. My preference is to collect only what I would enjoy, in or out of the box, regardless of what the doll will be worth in the future.

❊ ABOUT THE AUTHOR ❊

Maria Martinez-Esguerra's interest in Barbie dolls began when her neighbor gave her young daughter a brunette My First Barbie doll for a birthday present in 1990. On Christmas day that year, her daughter got two Dolls of the World Barbies from her grandparents! Ever since then, both mother and daughter have included Barbie dolls in their birthday and Christmas wish lists as well as in every shopping list! Daughter collects regular line Barbie dolls for play and pure enjoyment; mother collects exclusive dolls for investment. All of the dolls shown in this book are from their collection.

Maria graduated with business degrees from San Francisco State University and Golden Gate University in San Francisco, California. In her current vocation she is a full-time investigator, a part-time instructor, a Sunday school teacher, and mother to her nine-year-old daughter with whom she shares her avocation of collecting Barbie dolls, and photography. She has taken a short course in photography and also written and published a book of poetry. Each doll in this collection was photographed by Maria.

Maria currently resides in Fresno, California, with her childhood sweetheart, who is now her husband, and their daughter.

BLONDE BARBIE AND RED–HAIRED MIDGE

---------- ❧ ----------

1989, All Stars, blonde, #9099, $25.00.

---------- ❧ ----------

—————— ❀ ——————
1989, All Stars, Midge, #9360, $30.00.
—————— ❀ ——————

———— ✗❋ ————

1989, Barbie & the Beat,
blonde, #2751, $25.00.

———— ✗❋ ————

——— ⚹ ———
**1989, Barbie & the Beat,
Midge, #2752, $30.00.**
——— ⚹ ———

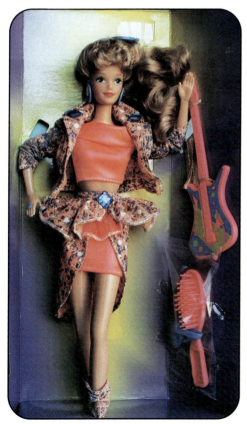

1989, Dance Magic, blonde, #4836, $25.00.

1989, Flight Time, blonde, #9584, $35.00.

1989, Fun To Dress, blonde, #4808, $15.00.

1989, Ice Capades, blonde
1st ed., #7365, $25.00.

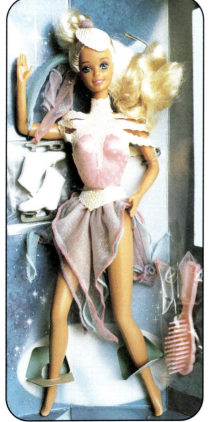

1989, My First Princess, blonde, #9942, $25.00.

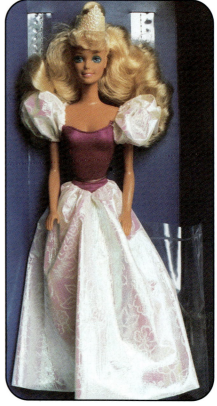

1989, Wedding Fantasy, blonde, #2125, $35.00.

1989, Western Fun, blonde, #9932, $30.00.

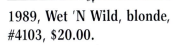

1989, Wet 'N Wild, blonde, #4103, $20.00.

————— ✻ —————

1990, All American, #9423, $25.00.

————— ✻ —————

1990, Bathtime Fun, blonde, #9601, $15.00.

—— ✂✻ ——

1990, Benetton, blonde, #9404, $35.00.

—— ✂✻ ——

1990, Costume Ball, blonde, #7123, $30.00.

———— ✿ ————

1990, Fashion Play, blonde, #9629, $15.00.

———— ✿ ————

———————— ✻ ————————
**1990, Happy Birthday,
blonde, #7913, $35.00.**
———————— ✻ ————————

1990, Hawaiian Fun, blonde, #5940, $18.00.

1990, Home Pretty, #2249, $25.00.

1990, Ice Capades, blonde
2nd ed., #9847, $30.00.

1990, Lights & Lace, blonde, #9725, $25.00.

1990, Wedding Day, Barbie, #9608, $25.00.

1990, Wedding Day, Midge, #9606, $30.00.

1991, American Beauty
Queen, #3137, $35.00.

—— ✻ ——

1991, Bath Magic, blonde, #5274, $15.00.

—— ✻ ——

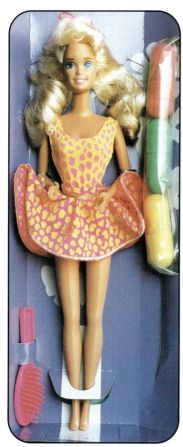

1991, Benetton Shopping, blonde, #4873, $30.00.

———————— ⚜ ————————
1991, Birthday Surprise,
blonde, #3679, $35.00.
———————— ⚜ ————————

1991, Dream Bride, #1623, $50.00.

——— ✕✱ ———
1991, Fashion Play, blonde, #2370, $15.00.
——— ✕✱ ———

1991, Mermaid, #1434, $25.00.

1991, My First Ballerina, blonde, #3839, $20.00.

1991, Pretty Surprise,
#9823, $25.00.

1991, Rappin' Rockin', blonde, #3248, $40.00.

———————— ⚘ ————————
1991, Rollerblade, blonde,
#2214, $35.00.
———————— ⚘ ————————

1991, Sharin' Sisters #1,
#5716, $40.00.

————————— ✗✱ —————————
1991, Ski Fun, blonde, #7511, $30.00.
————————— ✗✱ —————————

—— ❧ ——

1991, Ski Fun, Midge, #7513, $35.00.

—— ❧ ——

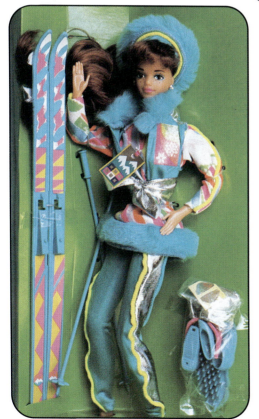

1991, Snap 'N Play, blonde, #3550, $20.00.

——— ❧✻ ———
1991, Sparkle Eyes,
blonde, #2482, $27.00.
——— ❧✻ ———

1991, Sun Sensation, blonde, #1390, $18.00.

1991, Teen Talk, blonde, #5745, $30.00.

1991, Teen Talk, redhead, #5745, $35.00.

——— ✹ ———

1991, Totally Hair, blonde,
#1112, $25.00.

——— ✹ ———

1992, Bath Blast, blonde, #4159, $15.00.

1992, Birthday Party, blonde, #3388, $35.00.

1992, Caboodles, #3157, $20.00.

⚬ᵡ⚬

1992, Earring Magic, blonde, #7014, $20.00.

⚬ᵡ⚬

1992, Earring Magic, Midge, #10256, $25.00.

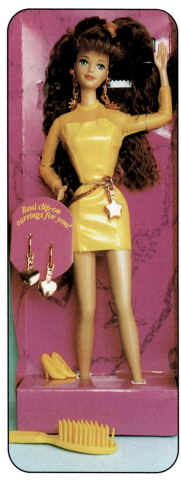

1992, Fun to Dress, blonde, #3826, $15.00.

—— ❧ ——

1992, Glitter Beach, blonde, #3602, $12.00.

—— ❧ ——

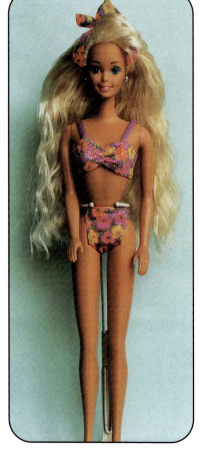

---✻---

1992, Hollywood Hair, blonde, #2308, $25.00.

---✻---

1992, My First Ballerina, blonde, #2516, $19.00.

—————— ✻ ——————
1992, Romantic Bride,
blonde, #1861, $35.00.
—————— ✻ ——————

———————— ✄❋ ————————

1992, Secret Hearts, blonde, #7902, $20.00.

———————— ✄❋ ————————

Make hearts magically appear on her dress!

1992, Sharin' Sisters #2,
#10143, $35.00.

1992, Troll, #10257, $20.00.

Mix & match
troll hair
for Barbie,
troll & you!

———————— ✂❋ ————————

1993, Bicycling, blonde #11689, $30.00.

———————— ✂❋ ————————

1993, Birthday, blonde, #11333, $30.00.

—————— ❧ ——————

1993, Camp, Midge, #11077, $20.00.

—————— ❧ ——————

1993, Camp, blonde, #11074, $20.00.

1993, Doctor, blonde, #11160, $30.00.

—————— ✣❋ ——————

1993, Dress 'N Fun, blonde, #10776, $15.00.

—————— ✣❋ ——————

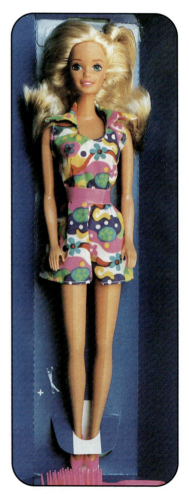

———————— ✶ ————————

1993, Fountain Mermaid, #10393, $20.00.

———————— ✶ ————————

1993, Glitter Hair, blonde, #10965, $15.00.

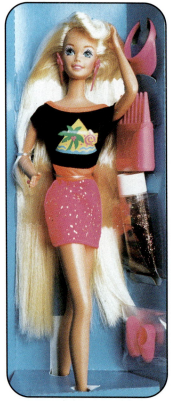

1993, Glitter Hair, redhead, #10968, $15.00.

1993, Gymnast, blonde, #12126, $15.00.

———— ❧ ————
1993, Locket Surprise, blonde, #10963, $20.00.
———— ❧ ————

1993, Locket Surprise, Kayla, #11209, $20.00.

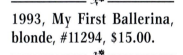

1993, My First Ballerina, blonde, #11294, $15.00.

1993, Paint 'N Dazzle, blonde, #10039, $20.00.

1993, Paint 'N Dazzle, red-head, #10057, $20.00.

———— ✳ ————

1993, Sun Jewel, blonde,
#10953, #10.00.

———— ✳ ————

1993, Swim 'n Dive, blonde, #11505, $20.00.

1993, Twinkle Lights, blonde, #10390, $25.00.

1993, Western Stampin',
blonde, #10293, $25.00.

1994, Baywatch, blonde,
#13199, $20.00.

1994, Birthday, blonde,
#12954, $25.00.

1994, Bubble Angel, blonde, #12443, $15.00.

————— ❀ —————

1994, Butterfly Princess, blonde, #13051, $25.00.

————— ❀ —————

1994, Cut 'N Style, blonde,
#12639, $15.00.

—————— ❧✴ ——————
**1994, Cut 'N Style, redhead,
#12644, $15.00.**
—————— ❧✴ ——————

1994, Dance Moves, blonde, #13083, $15.00.

1994, Dance Moves, Midge, #13085, $15.00.

1994, Dance & Twirl, blonde, #11902, $45.00.

———— ❀ ————

1994, Hot Skatin', blonde, #13511, $15.00.

———— ❀ ————

1994, Hot Skatin', Midge, #13393, $15.00.

✵

1994, My First Princess,
blonde, #13064, $15.00.

✵

1994, Ruffle Fun, blonde, #12433, $10.00.

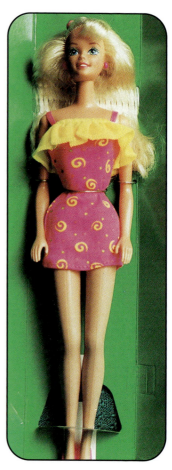

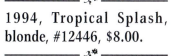

1994, Tropical Splash, blonde, #12446, $8.00.

——————— ✄❋ ———————
1995, Flying Hero, blonde, #14030, $15.00.
——————— ✄❋ ———————

—————— ✣ ——————

1995, Foam 'n Color, blue, #15099, $15.00.

—————— ✣ ——————

1995, Foam 'n Color, pink, #14457, $15.00.

—————— ✻ ——————
1995, Foam 'n Color, yellow,
#15098, $15.00.
—————— ✻ ——————

1995, Happy Birthday, blonde, #14649, $20.00.

1995, Jewel Hair Mermaid, Midge, #14589, $15.00.

1995, Jewel Hair Mermaid, blonde, #14586, $15.00.

—— ❧✻ ——
1995, My First Tea Party, blonde, #14592, $12.00.
—— ❧✻ ——

❋

1995, Olympic Gymnast, blonde, #15123, $15.00.

❋

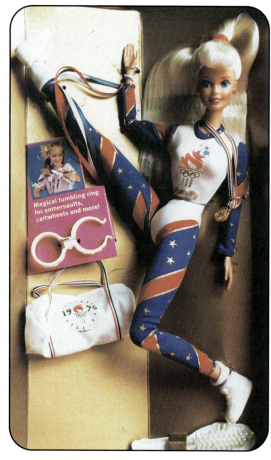

1995, Olympic Gymnast, redhead, #15125, $25.00.

1995, Pretty Hearts, blonde, #14473, $8.00.

—————— ❊ ——————

1995, Shopping Fun, blonde, #15756, $20.00.

—————— ❊ ——————

1995, Songbird, blonde, #14320, $20.00.

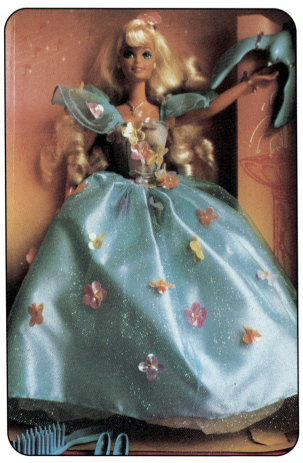

1995, Sparkle Beach, blonde, #13132, $8.00.

1995, Super Talk, blonde,
#14308, $25.00.

——— ✾ ———

1995, Teacher, blonde,
#13914, $25.00.

——— ✾ ———

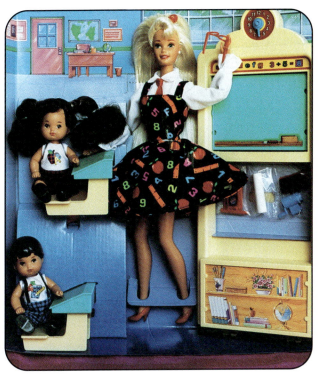

1995, Twirling Ballerina, blonde, #15086, $15.00.

1996, Angel Princess, blonde, #15911, $25.00.

1996, Birthday, blonde, #15998, $20.00.

1996, Blossom Beauty, blonde, #17032, $20.00.

1996, Bubblin' Mermaid, blonde, #16131, $15.00.

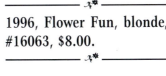

1996, Flower Fun, blonde, #16063, $8.00.

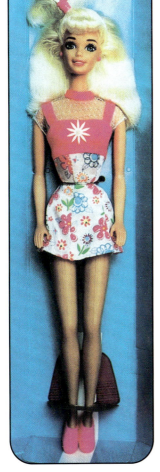

1996, Hula Hair, blonde, #17047, $15.00.

1996, My First Jewelry Fun,
blonde, #16005, $15.00.

———— ✻ ————
1996, Ocean Friends, blonde, #15428, $15.00.
———— ✻ ————

———— ❧✳ ————

1996, Pet Doctor, blonde, #14603, $20.00.

———— ❧✳ ————

1996, Splash 'n Color, blonde, #16169, $6.00.

1996, Workin' Out, blonde, #17317, $15.00.

1997, Barbie & Ginger, blonde, #17116, $35.00.

1997, Cool Shoppin', blonde, #17487, $20.00.

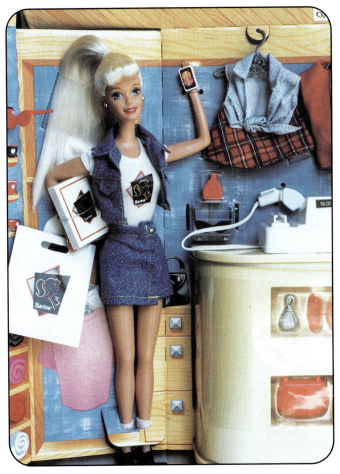

1997, Dentist, blonde, #17255, $20.00.

1997, Movin' Groovin', blonde, #17714, $15.00.

1997, Pearl Beach, blonde, #18576, $6.00.

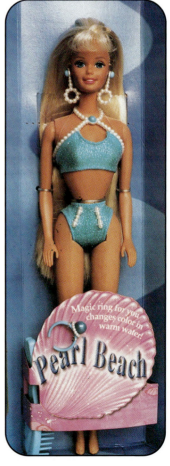

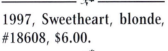

1997, Sweetheart, blonde, #18608, $6.00.

BRUNETTE BARBIE, HISPANIC TERESA, AND TARA LYNN

———— ❧ ————

1989, All Stars, Teresa, #9353, $30.00.

———— ❧ ————

1989, Flight Time, Hispanic, #2066, $35.00.

—— ⚘ ——

1989, Fun To Dress, Hispanic, #7373, $15.00.

—— ⚘ ——

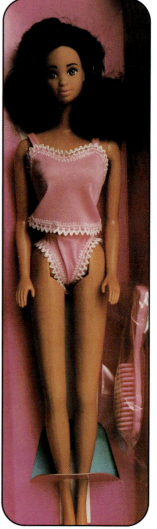

1989, My First Princess,
Hispanic, #9944, $25.00.

❦

1989, Wet 'n Wild, Teresa, #4136, $25.00.

❦

———————— ⚜ ————————

**1990, All American, Teresa,
#9426, $25.00.**

———————— ⚜ ————————

—— ✳ ——

1990, Fashion Play, Hispanic, #5954, $15.00.

—— ✳ ——

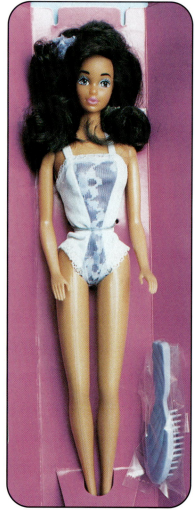

——— ❧✳ ———

1990, Lights & Lace, Teresa, #9727, $30.00.

——— ❧✳ ———

———— ⚹ ————

1991, Fashion Play, Hispanic,
#3860, $15.00.

———— ⚹ ————

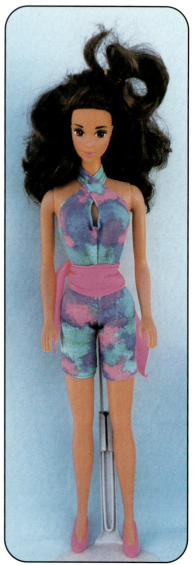

—— ❧ ——
1991, My First Ballerina,
Hispanic, #3864, $20.00.
—— ❧ ——

———— ✄ ————
1991, Rappin' Rockin',
Teresa, #3270, $45.00.
———— ✄ ————

1991, Rollerblade, Teresa, #2216, $40.00.

1991, Teen Talk, brunette, #5745, $35.00.

——— ❧ ———

1991, Totally Hair, brunette, #1117, $30.00.

——— ❧ ———

———— ✻ ————
1992, Earring Magic, brunette, #10255, $25.00.
———— ✻ ————

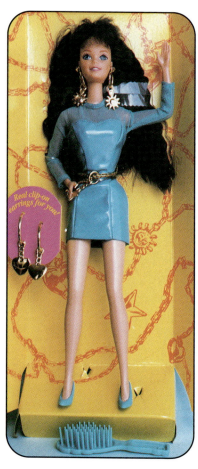

1992, Fun to Dress, Hispanic, #2763, $15.00.

——— ✳ ———

1992, Glitter Beach, Teresa, #4921, $12.00.

——— ✳ ———

———— ✻ ————
1992, Hollywood Hair,
Teresa, #2316, $30.00.
———— ✻ ————

✻

1992, My First Ballerina, Hispanic, #2770, $17.00.

✻

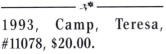

1993, Camp, Teresa, #11078, $20.00.

1993, Dress 'N Fun, Hispanic, #11102, $15.00.

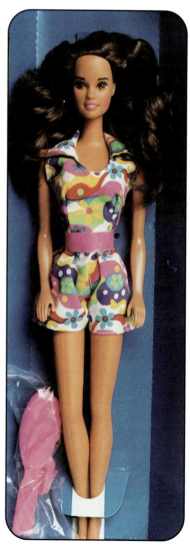

—— ✳ ——

1993, Glitter Hair, brunette, #10966, $15.00.

—— ✳ ——

1993, Paint 'N Dazzle, brunette, #10059, $20.00.

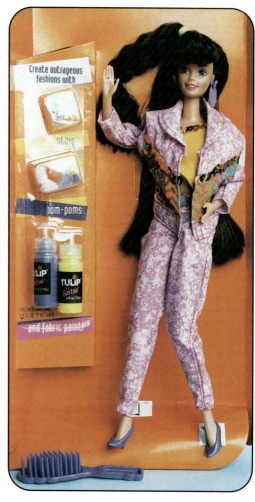

———— ✄ ————

1993, Sun Jewel, Teresa, #19057, $10.00.

———— ✄ ————

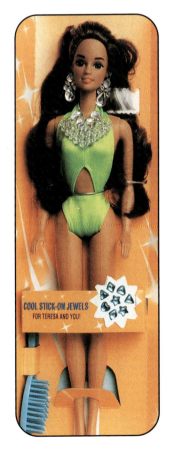

———— ⚹ ————
**1993, Western Stampin',
Tara Lynn, #10295, $45.00.**
———— ⚹ ————

1994, Baywatch, Teresa, #13201, $35.00.

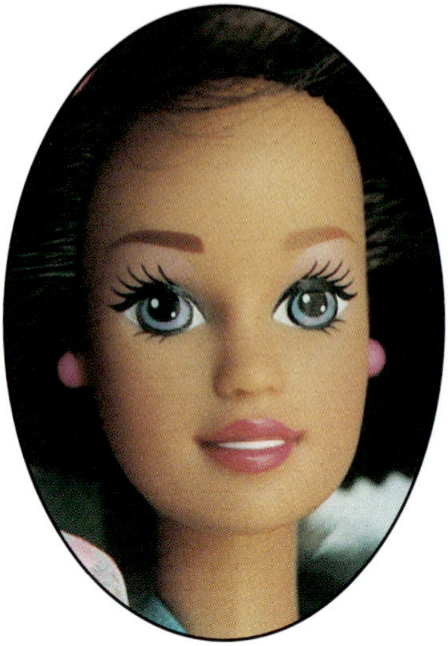

1994, Birthday, Hispanic, #13253, $25.00.

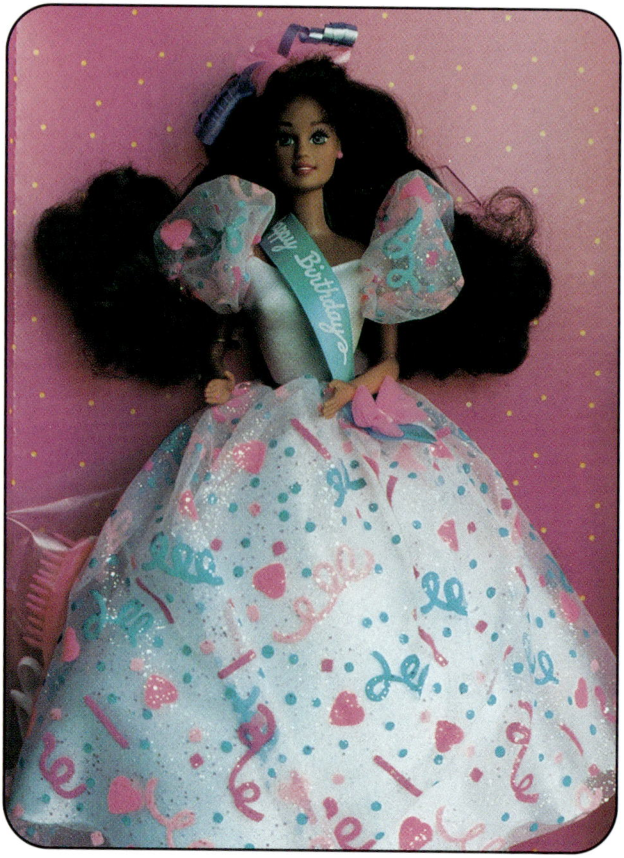

1994, Butterfly Princess,
Hispanic, #13238, $25.00.

1994, Cut 'N Style, brunette, #12643, $15.00.

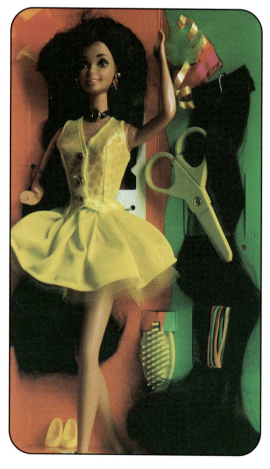

———— ✼ ————

1994, Dance Moves, Teresa,
#13084, $15.00.

———— ✼ ————

1994, My First Princess, Hispanic, #13066, $15.00.

❧
1994, Quinceanera, #11928, $30.00.

❧

1994, Ruffle Fun, Hispanic, #12435, $10.00.

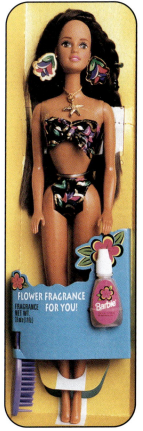

————— ✿ —————

1994, Tropical Splash, Teresa, #12450, $8.00.

————— ✿ —————

1995, Flying Hero, Teresa, #14031, $15.00.

1995, Happy Birthday, Hispanic, #14663, $20.00.

1995, Jewel Hair Mermaid,
Teresa, #14588, $15.00.

Sparkly stars for hair styling fun!

———— ✣ ————
1995, My First Tea Party,
Hispanic, #14875, $12.00.
———— ✣ ————

1995, Pretty Hearts, Hispanic, #14475, $8.00.

—— ⚹⁕ ——

1995, Songbird, Teresa, #14484, $20.00.

—— ⚹⁕ ——

1995, Sparkle Beach, Teresa, #14354, $8.00.

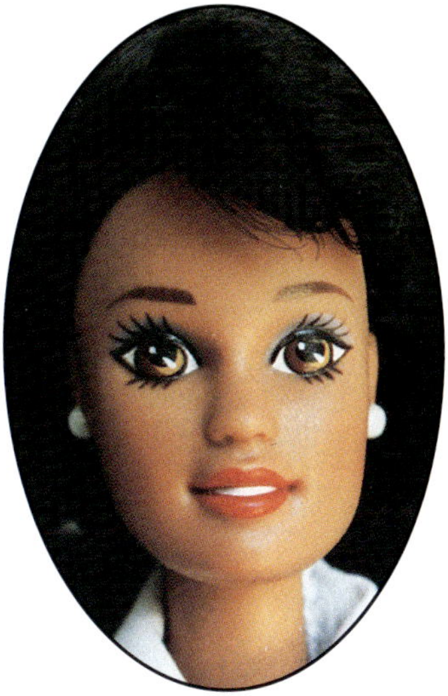

1995, Teacher, Hispanic, #16210, $25.00.

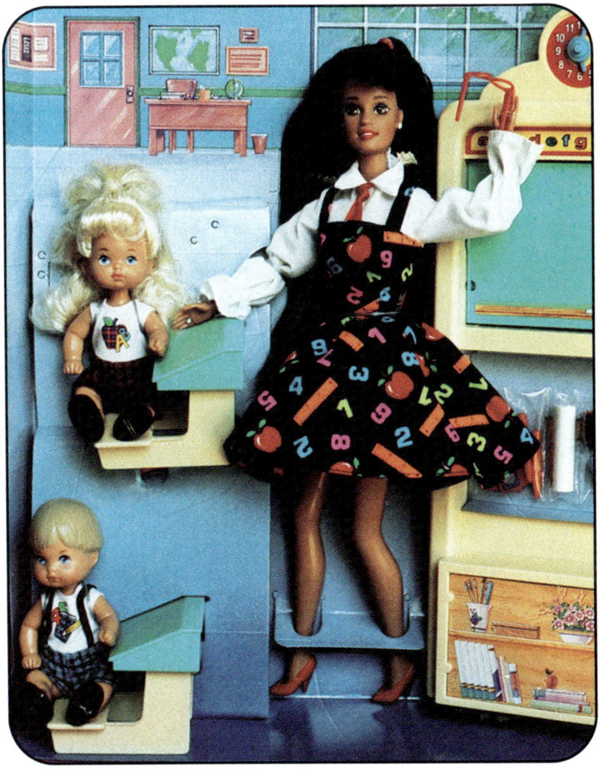

1995, Twirling Ballerina, Teresa, #15299, $15.00.

1996, Birthday, Hispanic, #16000, $20.00.

1996, Blossom Beauty, Teresa, #17035, $20.00.

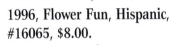

1996, Flower Fun, Hispanic, #16065, $8.00.

— ⅔❋ —

1996, Hula Hair, Teresa, #17049, $15.00.

— ⅔❋ —

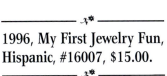

1996, My First Jewelry Fun, Hispanic, #16007, $15.00.

—— ✻ ——

**1996, Pet Doctor, brunette,
#16458, $25.00.**

—— ✻ ——

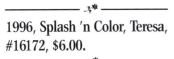

1996, Splash 'n Color, Teresa, #16172, $6.00.

1996, Workin' Out, Teresa, #17318, $15.00.

1997, Dentist, brunette, #17707, $20.00.

1997, Movin' Groovin', Teresa, #17716, $15.00.

❧ ✲

1997, Pearl Beach, Teresa,
#18579, $6.00.

❧ ✲

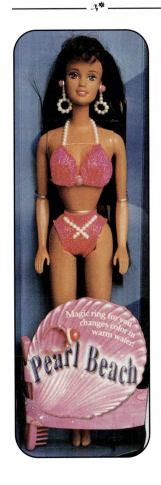

———— ✾ ————

1997, Sweetheart, brunette,
#18610, $6.00.

———— ✾ ————

1989, All Stars, Christie, #9352, $25.00.

1989, Barbie & the Beat,
Christie, #2754, $25.00.

——————— ✲✳ ———————
1989, Dance Magic, black,
#7080, $25.00.
——————— ✲✳ ———————

1989, Flight Time, black, #9916, $35.00.

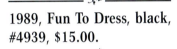

1989, Fun To Dress, black, #4939, $15.00.

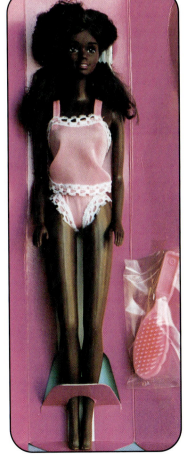

1989, Ice Capades, black 1st ed., #7348, $25.00.

1989, My First Princess, black, #9943, $25.00.

1989, Wedding Fantasy, black, #7011, $35.00.

—————— ✾ ——————

1989, Western Fun, black, #2930, $30.00.

—————— ✾ ——————

1989, Wet 'n Wild, Christie, #4121, $20.00.

———————— ✂❋ ————————

1990, All American, Christie, #9425, $25.00.

———————— ✂❋ ————————

1990, Bathtime Fun, black, #9603, $15.00.

———— ❧ ————

1990, Benetton, Christie, #9407, $35.00.

———— ❧ ————

1990, Costume Ball, black, #7134, $30.00.

1990, Fashion Play, black, #5953, $15.00.

1990, Happy Birthday, black, #9561, $35.00.

———— ✻ ————
1990, Hawaiian Fun,
Christie, #5944, $18.00.
———— ✻ ————

———— ✂✻ ————
1990, Lights & Lace,
Christie, #9728, $25.00.
———— ✂✻ ————

—— ✳ ——
1991, American Beauty
Queen, black, #3245, $35.00.
—— ✳ ——

1991, Bath Magic, black, #7951, $15.00.

1991, Birthday Surprise, black, #4051, $35.00.

1991, Fashion Play, black, #3842, $15.00.

1991, My First Ballerina, black, #3861, $20.00.

1991, Rappin' Rockin', Christie, #3265, $45.00.

1991, Rollerblade, Christie, #2217, $35.00.

1991, Snap 'N Play, black, #3556, $20.00.

1991, Sparkle Eyes, black, #5950, $27.00.

1991, Sun Sensation, Christie, #1393, $18.00.

1991, Teen Talk, black, #1612, $30.00.

1991, Totally Hair, black, #5948, $25.00.

1992, Bath Blast, black, #3830, $15.00.

1992, Birthday Party, black, #7948, $35.00.

1992, Earring Magic, black, #2374, $20.00.

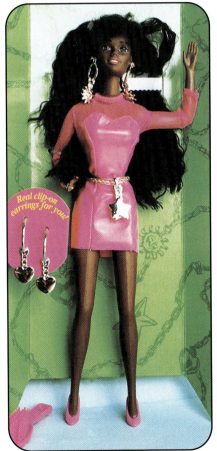

———— ⚜ ————

1992, Fun To Dress, black, #2570, $15.00.

———— ⚜ ————

1992, Glitter Beach, Christie, #4907, $12.00.

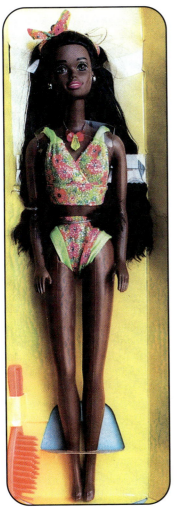

1992, My First Ballerina, black, #2767, $17.00.

1992, Romantic Bride,
black, #1861, $35.00.

1992, Secret Hearts, black, #3836, $20.00.

1993, Bicycling, black, #11817, $30.00.

1993, Birthday, black, #11334, $30.00.

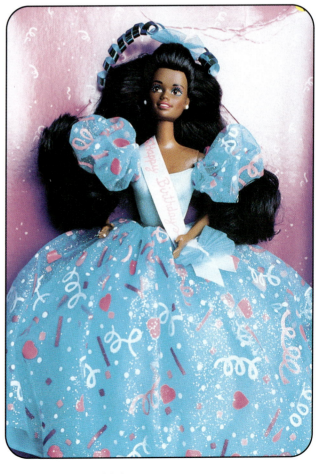

———————— 🌿❀ ————————
1993, Camp, black, #11831,
$20.00.
———————— 🌿❀ ————————

1993, Doctor, black, #11814, $30.00.

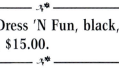

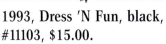

1993, Dress 'N Fun, black, #11103, $15.00.

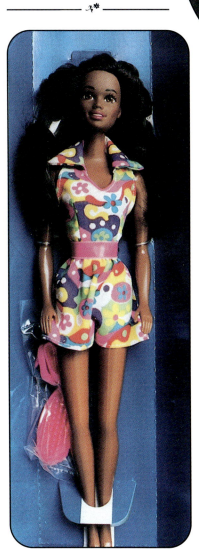

1993, Fountain Mermaid, black, #10522, $20.00.

1993, Glitter Hair, black, #11332, $15.00.

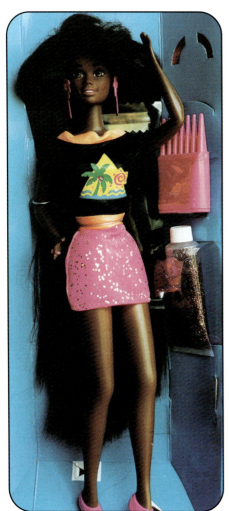

1993, Locket Surprise, black, #11224, $20.00.

1993, My First Ballerina, black, #11340, $15.00.

1993, Paint 'N Dazzle, black, #10058, $20.00.

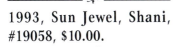

1993, Sun Jewel, Shani, #19058, $10.00.

1993, Swim 'n Dive, black, #11734, $20.00.

1993, Twinkle Lights, black, #10521, $25.00.

1993, Western Stampin', black, #10539, $25.00.

1994, Baywatch, black, #13258, $20.00.

1994, Birthday, black, #12955, $25.00.

1994, Bubble Angel, black, #12444, $15.00.

1994, Butterfly Princess, black, #13052, $25.00.

1994, Cut 'N Style, black, #12642, $15.00.

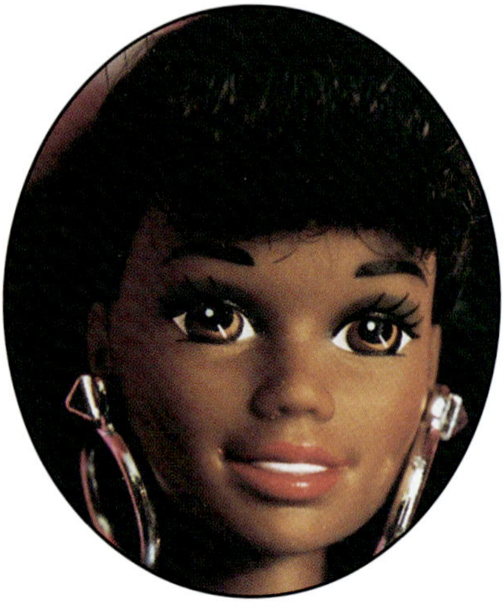

1994, Dance Moves, black, #13086, $15.00.

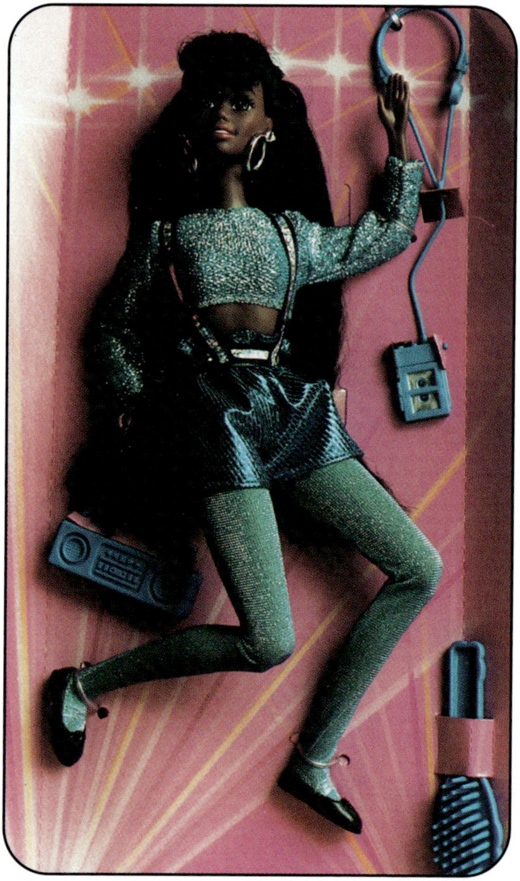

—— ✕✱ ——

1994, Dance & Twirl, black, #12143, $45.00.

—— ✕✱ ——

———— ✂ ————
1994, Gymnast, black,
#12153, $15.00.
———— ✂ ————

—————— ✿ ——————
1994, Hot Skatin', black, #13512, $15.00.
—————— ✿ ——————

1994, My First Princess, black, #13065, $15.00.

—— ❧ ——
1994, Ruffle Fun, black,
#12434, $10.00.
—— ❧ ——

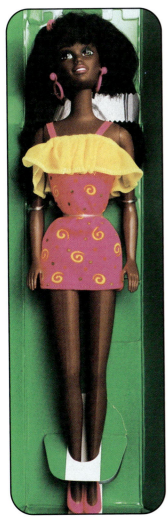

1994, Tropical Splash, Christie, #12451, $8.00.

—— ✶❋ ——
1995, Flying Hero, black, #14278, $15.00.
—— ✶❋ ——

1995, Happy Birthday, black, #14662, $20.00.

———— ✳ ————

1995, Jewel Hair Mermaid,
black, #14587, $15.00.

———— ✳ ————

Sparkly stars for hair styling fun!

1995, My First Tea Party, black, #14593, $12.00.

1995, Olympic Gymnast, black, #15124, $15.00.

1995, Pretty Hearts, black, #14474, $8.00.

1995, Shopping Fun, black, #15757, $20.00.

1995, Songbird, black, #14486, $20.00.

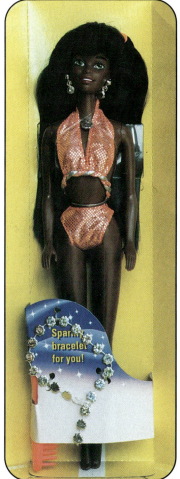

—— ✿ ——

1995, Sparkle Beach, Christie, #14355, $8.00.

—— ✿ ——

1995, Super Talk, black, #1675, $25.00.

——— ❧ ———
1995, Teacher, black,
#13915, $25.00.
——— ❧ ———

1995, Twirling Ballerina, black, #15087, $15.00.

1996, Angel Princess, black, #15912, $25.00.

1996, Birthday, black, #15999, $20.00.

1996, Blossom Beauty, black, #17033, $20.00.

———— ✿ ————

1996, Flower Fun, black, #16064, $8.00.

———— ✿ ————

1996, Hula Hair, ethnic, #17048, $15.00.

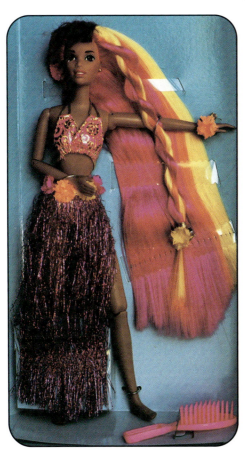

1996, My First Jewelry Fun, black, #16006, $15.00.

1996, Ocean Friends, black, #15429, $15.00.

1996, Pet Doctor, black, #15302, $20.00.

1996, Splash 'n Color, Christie, #16174, $6.00.

271

1996, Workin' Out, Christie, #17319, $15.00.

—— ✿ ——

1997, Barbie & Ginger, black, #17369, $35.00.

—— ✿ ——

1997, Cool Shoppin', black, #17488, $20.00.

———————— ⚘ ————————

1997, Dentist, black, #17478,
$20.00.

———————— ⚘ ————————

1997, Movin' Groovin',
Christie, #17715, $15.00.

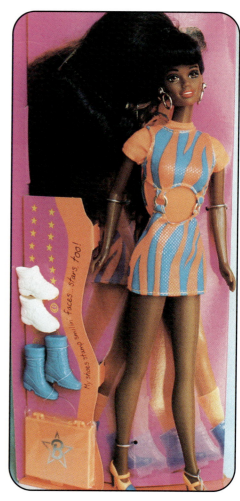

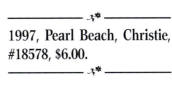

1997, Pearl Beach, Christie, #18578, $6.00.

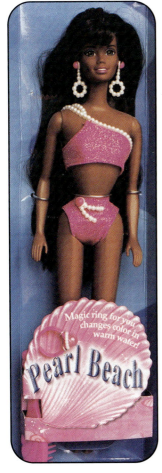

—— ✿ ——

1997, Sweetheart, black, #18609, $6.00.

—— ✿ ——

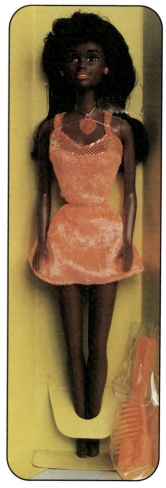

ASIAN AND NATIVE AMERICAN BARBIE, KIRA, AND NIA

1989, Western Fun, Nia, #9933, $45.00.

1989, Wet 'n Wild, Kira, #4120, $20.00.

1990, All American, Kira, #9427, $25.00.

1990, Benetton, Kira, #9409, $35.00.

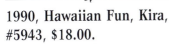

1990, Hawaiian Fun, Kira, #5943, $18.00.

1991, Rollerblade, Kira, #2218, $35.00.

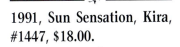

1991, Sun Sensation, Kira,
#1447, $18.00.

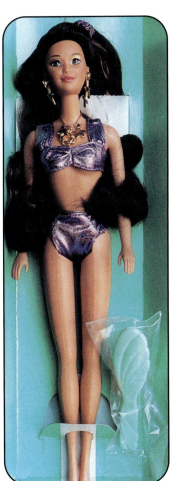

———— ≈❋ ————
1992, Glitter Beach, Kira,
#4924, $12.00.
———— ≈❋ ————

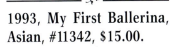

1993, My First Ballerina, Asian, #11342, $15.00.

1993, Sun Jewel, Kira, #19056, $10.00.

1994, My First Princess, Asian, #13067, $15.00.

1994, Tropical Splash, Kira, #12449, $8.00.

1995, Flying Hero, Kira, #14032, $15.00.

1995, My First Tea Party, Asian, #14876, $12.00.

1995, Sparkle Beach, Kira, #14351, $8.00.

1996, My First Jewelry Fun, Asian, #16008, $15.00.

—————— ⚜ ——————
1996, Ocean Friends, Kira,
#15431, $15.00.
—————— ⚜ ——————

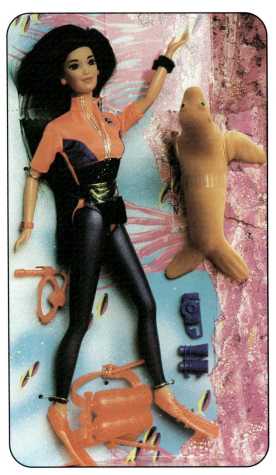

1996, Splash 'n Color, Kira, #16173, $6.00.

1997, Movin' Groovin', Kira, #17717, $15.00.

1997, Pearl Beach, Kira, #18580, $6.00.

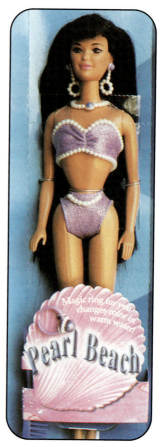

❖ CHRONOLOGICAL INDEX ❖